D1551535

# College Scholarships for High School Credit

## Learn and Earn with this Two-for-One Strategy

## Lee Binz,
### The HomeScholar

© 2018 by **The HomeScholar LLC**

All Rights Reserved. No part of this publication may be reproduced in any form or by any means, including scanning, photocopying, or otherwise without prior written permission of the copyright holder.

First Printing, 2018

Printed in the United States of America

Cover Design by Robin Montoya
Edited by Kimberly Charron

ISBN: 1724584898
ISBN-13: 978-1724584892

**Disclaimer:** Parents assume full responsibility for the education of their children in accordance with state law. College requirements vary, so make sure to check with the colleges about specific requirements for homeschoolers. We offer no guarantees, written or implied, that the use of our products and services will result in college admissions or scholarship awards.

# College Scholarships for High School Credit

## Learn and Earn with this Two-for-One Strategy

# What are Coffee Break Books?

*College Scholarships for High School Credit* is part of The HomeScholar's Coffee Break Book series.

Designed especially for parents who don't want to spend hours and hours reading a 400-page book on homeschooling high school, each book combines Lee's practical and friendly approach with detailed, but easy-to-digest information, perfect to read over a cup of coffee at your favorite coffee shop!

Never overwhelming, always accessible and manageable, each book in the series will give parents the tools they need to tackle the tasks of homeschooling high school, one warm sip at a time.

Everything about these Coffee Break Books is designed to connote simplicity, ease and comfort—from the size (fits in a purse), to the font and paragraph length (easy on the eyes), to the price (the same as a Starbucks Venti Triple Caramel Macchiato). Unlike a fancy coffee drink, however, these books are guilt-free pleasures you will want to enjoy again and again!

# Table of Contents

Introduction

# Two Birds with One Stone

If you're like the typical homeschool family, you probably don't have a huge sum of money put away for your children's college costs. Somehow, raising a family on a single income nowadays doesn't leave a lot left over for college tuition funds! Applying for scholarships is one of the best ways to make up for the shortfall, so while they were juniors, we encouraged our sons to apply for many college scholarships.

Of course, applying for scholarships takes a lot of time, so to do this on top of their regular schoolwork would have been a burden. Therefore, we tried to kill two birds with one stone and found private scholarships our children wrote essays for or completed educational activities to fulfill a requirement. Afterwards, we counted those essays or educational activities for high school credit.

I discovered that essay writing was something my children did well, so during junior year I started to search for scholarships and used their writing for high school English credit that year. I noticed that small scholarships led to bigger scholarships. A small scholarship was included on their activities and awards list, which then led to larger scholarships from colleges.

Private scholarships may yield less money than the scholarships from colleges, but they are still a great way for your curriculum to pay you instead of the other way around. The best way to win private scholarships is to use a rigorous curriculum throughout high school and to teach your child to write well. A good vocabulary and essay writing skills will help when it comes to writing essays.

If your child isn't writing well, focus more on artistic and hands-on scholarships. Your child's unique interests (see chapter 7) can help you find scholarships that are completely tailored to your child.

In the following pages, we'll cover the steps to winning private scholarships, including *finding* scholarships, *filtering* them, *formatting* them so they're easy to fill out, *following through* (the hard part), and *filing* the educational experience in your educational record. Let's begin!

Chapter 1

# How to Win Private Scholarships: Find

If you search "college scholarships" on Google, you'll get about 365 million hits! As much as you'd like to think 365 million scholarships would be a wonderful thing, it is not humanly possible to apply for that many scholarships, even over four years of college and certainly not in one year of college or high school. Instead, use a search engine specifically for scholarships. Good ones to try are www.fastweb.com, www.collegenet.com, www.finaid.org, www.edfinancial.com, and www.scholarships.com. Some scholarships are unique to specific states, so try Googling your state and the word "scholarship" and see what shows up.

After you log on to a scholarship site, the first thing to do is input information about your student. The more you tell them about your student, the more tailored to them the scholarship search will be. As much as this seems counter intuitive, you need to narrow the scholarships down to ones your child is qualified for. It's impossible to apply for 400 scholarships anyway, so the best way to filter them is to input your student's information.

This takes a long time. When you're filling these out for the first time, allow yourself at least two hours to input information. This narrows the possibilities from 6.5 million hits to a few hundred. If each scholarship takes a week to apply to, and there are only 36 weeks of school, it doesn't add up! Even if your child worked all year round, they still couldn't apply for four hundred scholarships. You need to keep it down to maybe 30 or 40 scholarships to apply to throughout the year.

In addition to scholarship search engines, look over scholarships won by family and friends, other high school students, and scholarships available through local businesses. When our sons were in their senior year of high school, I was surprised by how many scholarships I saw on store walls. Be open to the different avenues through which you might hear about scholarships.

Looking for college scholarships takes a lot of time, but it's well worth it. After all, who doesn't want free money for college?! We searched our local high school's scholarship databases. School districts often have an entire page devoted to scholarships. Another method we pursued was to Google the words "scholarship" along with words that described our sons' areas of specialization, such as "chess" or "economics."

Only spend your energy pursuing scholarships your child is qualified for. Like baseball, it can be boiled down to one statement: "One strike and you're out." As you look at a scholarship, the moment you see a requirement or preference that eliminates your child, give up on that scholarship and move on. It doesn't matter how much you want that $20,000, if it says it's only for girls and you have a boy, you're out! You may have a hundred scholarships to weed through, so you don't have time to argue about how your child should be allowed to apply.

Eliminate the scholarship immediately as well if it requires skills your child does not have. For instance, it would have been lovely for my son to apply for a scholarship that involved making a YouTube video about economics. Unfortunately, although he knew economics, he didn't know how to create a video for YouTube!

Once you're this far and have filtered out all the scholarships your student is not qualified for, read the fine print. Check the details to see if, for instance, there's an exclusion for homeschoolers. This rarely happens, but you want to find this out before you fill out the application. Next, make a cost/benefit analysis. Sometimes the smaller essays are easier to win, so smaller ones might be better for your student to pursue. Local scholarships can also be easier to win because they have fewer applicants.

Something else to keep in mind is how much work an application will take versus how much money your child might get for it. If it requires a 3,000-word essay on a topic your child doesn't love and they're only awarding $50, it may not be worth it. On the other hand, if it's a 150-word poem and the monetary reward is $2,000, it might be worth it. Weigh your child's interest versus the motivation to fill it out.

Chapter 2

# How to Win Private Scholarships: Format

Searching for college scholarships is an incredibly time-consuming process. The more organized you are, the more likely your student is to win a scholarship. After all, the application that never gets turned in won't win any money! Keeping track of the many scholarships your child is working on is a major factor in college scholarship success and organization is key.

I kept information on each scholarship I found on Fastweb in a notebook. I printed out the application itself and sometimes printed essays written by previous winners, so my children could see what a winning essay looked like. I arranged scholarships in order of due date, with the most immediate due date first. I also created a separate page for each scholarship with everything my child needed to do. The page included scholarship information, the dollar amount of the scholarship (which was like dangling a carrot in front of their faces), what was required (an essay or letter), word count, and the due date. I set my due date way ahead of the prescribed due date, so my students got it done well before the *drop dead* due date!

Another important factor when working on scholarships is to estimate the time required to complete the application. As your child develops their writing skills during the earlier years of high school, pay attention to how much time it takes them to write an essay. For my children to write a good paper, they needed a whole week, which included brainstorming, writing, editing, and re-editing. They seemed able to generate about 500 to 1,000 words per week from start to finish.

In addition to writing a general essay, sometimes students need time to complete an application or other activities required, such as helping the elderly and writing about their experience. They may also need time to solicit letters of recommendation or to submit a transcript. A transcript is not something that can be whipped up in an hour and letters of recommendation don't materialize out of thin air. They'll need time to decide who they should ask to write the recommendation and time to get it before the scholarship deadline. Good organization is your best friend in this process and there's no better time to begin than now!

Chapter 3

# How to Win Private Scholarships: Follow Through

Ask any parent what the hardest part of working on scholarships is, and they will probably tell you it's getting their student to follow through on the application. You have control over finding and preparing scholarships but little control over follow through. Your student needs to do the work of writing the essays and getting the letters out, so this they can be the weakest link. Fortunately, there are steps you can follow to make everything flow more smoothly, even if you can't control the whole process.

First, make sure you and your child read the application thoroughly because there may be details you must attend to. For example, if an application requires you to include a transcript and it transcript isn't ready yet, that will be a problem. Keep track of all the details. For instance, you might be asked to mail a letter of recommendation separately with your student's phone number on it. Disregarding the details may end up in automatic disqualification.

Make sure to apply on time and accurately to all scholarships. After I finished homeschooling, I joined the board of my local homeschool organization and chaired the scholarship committee. When we received the first few applications, I wanted those students to win because they turned their applications in early, while the students who turned theirs in later did not impress me with their timeliness. So, apply on time and as early as possible.

Your student should be the one writing the essay and doing the projects, but after they've done so, it's a good time for you to go back and review previous winners. Consider the tone, voice, content, and format of previous winners (which is a good skill to teach your child before they go to college). If the winning essays are in the first or third person, that's the point of view they want. If the essay has a youthful tone with sassy or immature statements, then that's the kind of writing they're looking for. If the content of previous winners has an extremely liberal bias, that's the kind of writing they're looking for.

It's even important to look at the *format* of winning essays. Are they in 12-point Times New Roman font? Did they justify the document or was it simply aligned left? Make sure your student's is as similar as possible in format but unique in content. That uniqueness is why your student should write the application first, so they are not biased by what they see from the winners. After your child has written an essay, look at the previous winners.

## Application Form

Complete the application form with your child. You'd be surprised by what your children do and do not know and it's a great teaching opportunity. It's okay for you to edit each essay as you would an English paper in your homeschool. In addition, make sure to follow through. Read the details carefully because each one is important. Submit early and keep your focus on learning. As part of your homeschool, this activity is not only for the money, it's for learning, too. My children once wrote essays on osteoporosis and learned a lot about this health condition as a result. If you focus on learning and not only on winning, you will win in the overall game.

## In the End

Even when you follow through perfectly and submit early, your child may not win the scholarship—even if you know it's a perfect fit! I know this because it happened to us. We found the perfect scholarship essay for my son and he wrote a gorgeous essay, but he didn't win. Sometimes only one winner is chosen. If five perfect fit applicants apply and the evaluators must choose one winner, your child has a one-in-five chance of winning. Keep trying and don't get discouraged by the losses; there may be a win out there!

Chapter 4

# How to Win Private Scholarships: File

Much of the work your high school student does in pursuit of college scholarships can and should be counted as high school credit on their transcript. The typical high school junior or senior can spend hours on scholarship applications, so they deserve to receive credit for their work.

All the essays or other work your student produces should be saved in print form but save it on your computer as well. Create a file on your desktop titled "scholarships" or "schoolwork" and save their work there. You'll be able to use the same essays later, for different purposes. Whenever your student accrues 120 to 180 hours of work, they can earn a high school credit. If they're writing essays as well as reading for them for about one hour a day, you can count it as an English credit.

Instead of an English credit, your student might earn credit for a specialized course. For example, if your student loves a subject such as economics, and they fill up application essay after application essay on economics, then they may have learned a whole economics credit. For scholarships that require photography or artwork, your student may accrue quite a few art hours, which you can incorporate into an art class.

Sometimes homeschoolers forget that photography is an art. It was an art class at my public high school. Most photography is digital now, which appeals to the *techie* student. Add those hours together and incorporate them into your student's curriculum.

Determine grades for these hours the usual way, by evaluating what they did and determining grading criteria for each paper or project they worked on. Each essay might also get a grade for completion or research. Some papers my children produced didn't receive a good grade but were the ones that ended up earning scholarships. If this happens, you might want to go back and give your student an A for the paper, because somebody else graded it and thought it was good. If your student wins something with their work, give it an *A*.

In addition to including your child's work as credit, put anything they win on their activities and awards list. Even if they're only mentioned as a commended student, include it on their awards list.

Chapter 5

# Winning Benefits

So, your child applies to multiple college scholarship competitions and works hard. What if they don't win? Sometimes students do win. Your child might win money for college (most students' goal), or a gift certificate they can use to stock up for college. Even if they don't win money, there are some non-monetary benefits of winning. When your child wins and gets recommended, you can add it to their activities and awards list.

It's important to remember that even if they earn an award that doesn't have many monetary benefits (or none), a small award can lead to bigger awards. For example, my child won a $25 award from the Veterans of Foreign Wars, which put him in the running for the next bigger competition. This small award was the first step to winning a bigger reward.

Winning can have non-monetary benefits when an award leads to being published. Our eldest son won an essay award and was published in a collection of poems. The youngest wrote an essay on economics, which was published in *Liberty Magazine*.

Winning benefits might not include much money but may earn high school credit. Your children learn a lot on each subject they're writing about. Essay writing can be an inexpensive English program. It's an opportunity for your children to practice their writing skills. They learn how to read, follow detailed directions, and all about filling out application forms. This provides experience with concrete and inflexible deadlines.

I know many parents worry about how to get their child to turn things in, but scholarship application deadlines are completely concrete and inflexible, much like Tax Day. If you don't get it in, you don't get the money. This process can help your child practice their project manager skills because they know that they need to get their assignments done on time or else they won't win the money. Applications can also help parents realize they need to complete their student's transcript, and can be good motivators, too.

My favorite non-winning benefit is the opportunity to use and re-use essays. One of the most common scholarship essay topics is "What are your goals in life?" or a variant of this topic. It's difficult for kids to come up with long-term goals, because they're thinking, "Ice cream on Sunday would be good," and long-term is difficult for them. Keep all their application essays. When your child applies to college, remind them,

"Here's one you wrote about how to solve long term problems in engineering." They can re-use these essays, even years later.

Three years after my children wrote college scholarship essays for high school credit, we went back into their file and re-used one of their essays for a different scholarship later in college. The same applies to letters of recommendation. Once they have a letter, it's easy to go back to the same person and say a year later, "Remember when you wrote a letter of recommendation for me? Do you think you could freshen it up and write one again for this college?" It's easier for them to update it than start from the beginning.

Keeping work throughout your child's homeschool career can also help. My son filled out an application for a scholarship and wrote an essay. He received a reply that they wanted a short story, so he wrote a short story about children. He went back and read some of the winning entries from the past and learned that they didn't want a children's story. What they were looking for was a children's poem. All the previous winners had written poems, and most of them rhymed. My son decided not to write anything new at all; he didn't want to be bothered. Instead, he went back to his educational file on the computer and found a poem he had written in 5th grade. He cut and pasted it into a new Word document and submitted it to the scholarship program. He won.

As a winner of this scholarship, he received a $50 gift certificate to a bookstore. However, the bookstore took all the winning essays and published them into a book. Because my son was now published, the non-winning benefit of the whole process was 11 copies of the book. I sent a copy of the book to each of the colleges where he applied! Colleges are impressed when a student is a published author, whether it's in a book, magazine, or online! Even if your child doesn't win money, there are other benefits to winning awards!

Chapter 6

# Demonstration of Finding and Filtering

In this chapter, we will practice the find and filter aspect of looking for scholarships. Using Fastweb, you'll learn how to complete the profile and keep notes from each section as you go through. We'll cover filtering, how to remove any scholarship that isn't perfect, using the one-strike-you're-out rule, and then arrange them by due date.

Check out the Fastweb website. When you first log in, you will be asked to fill out a profile. Even after you've filled it out, you can still edit it by clicking on "My Profile." The first time you fill out your profile, they will ask questions such as: "Are you a high school junior?" and

"Are you looking for scholarships for a college freshman?" Type in the different colleges your child is interested in. If your child is interested in archaeology, type in "archeology" for career objectives.

For educational experience, there is a place to put "homeschooled," either currently or previously. I also added "honor student," even though we were homeschooling independently and didn't give AP courses, because I wanted to get access to some of the tougher academic scholarships. Academic honors is something you may not have unless your child is going to community college. After you fill out this section, hit "submit."

In addition to educational questions, the site will ask you about personal qualities such as disabilities and heritage. Don't discount anything. Look through the disability list. If your child has arthritis or ADD, make note of it. Don't hesitate to add this information because it could lead to more scholarship options.

When you are asked about sports, you can include what your student does for fun. It doesn't have to be a serious sport where only varsity applies. Look carefully through the personal attributes and think about each one. Some may be personal things you don't normally tell people, such as that your child is adopted. While it may seem as if some of them are unimportant, they could be important for a scholarship.

You will also be asked about student activities. This is where activities like 4-H Club come in. You need to remember what your child has done in the past. Make sure to read over each activity because each one is important and may prompt your memory.

Some questions will be about memberships—not only for the student, but also for the parents. They may ask you, "Is the parent employed by the 3M Company?" or "Are they a member of the Air Force?" They may ask, "Are you a member of the Teamsters?" and "Has your parent ever gone to college?" because there are scholarships only for children in these situations.

Filling out the profile can take hours. When you're all done, click on the place where it says "scholarships," or where it says, "see your scholarship matches now."

To figure out when each scholarship is due, look at the top where it says "Deadline." The scholarships will show up in the order they're due. When you look at your matches in order of due date, you'll notice they don't include scholarships evenly throughout the year. Most of them tend to be due in the first half of the year, so make sure you check back repeatedly. You have a high school student, not a college student!

When a scholarship says that it's available to high school students, it doesn't mean it's only available to public high school students; it's also available to homeschoolers (unless otherwise stated).

Fastweb does have a few drawbacks: many advertisements and emails. Based on the data you input, they'll send you emails such as, "We just got a new scholarship and we think that you're going to like it. It only requires a video and we think that you can do it." Even though they do bug you with advertising, it's a worthwhile site.

As you look for scholarships, make sure to use sites that are specific. Use the find, filter, one-strike-you're-out, format method, summarize each one, and organize by due date. The follow through is the important thing; details matter. Work on compliance with your children because your work isn't going to help if your student doesn't do the job of applying. Lastly, count all the work they do on scholarships toward high school credits, such as English credit for writing essays and fine arts credit for creating videos.

Chapter 7

# Delight Directed Learning for High School Credit

Some students aren't textbook people! What do you do if your homeschooler learns by living instead of studying textbooks? What if your child soaks up knowledge like a sponge, without being directed in any way? Can you still create a serious-looking high school transcript?

My son, Alex, was a self-motivated extreme learner. If only it were an Olympic event like extreme sports! He learned to write a novel for fun and wanted to take a third year of French even though I didn't have a curriculum for him. He asked for an American

government curriculum for Christmas
and read every economics book he could
get his hands on. Although his *love
language* is reading, he was still a
delight directed learner. When it was
time to make his transcript, I still had to
figure out how to translate his
experiences onto a piece of paper.

This problem seemed huge. What
should I do with all the experiences that
covered a wide range of subjects? Was
the report on Jean-Baptiste Say (the
French Economist) a paper on history,
economics, or foreign language? Was my
son Kevin's enjoyment of Russian
History just part of World History, or
could it be a course by itself? My
children wrote *so* many papers, but I
didn't know what subject I should
attribute them to!

**The Sticky Note Strategy**

I eventually found a system that could
help me sort out all my kids' delight

directed learning, using my understanding of traditional grades and credits. It's not difficult once you get the hang of it. Once I figured out how to do it, I realized that my system would work for *all* delight directed learners, not only *book learners*. I also realized that it could help parents who are kinesthetic learners.

My strategy is simple, fun, and only requires one small purchase—sticky notes. Those small, square notes save the day again! You can determine what to do with each experience using a simple sticky note.

For each activity your student is involved in, there are five pieces of information you need to remember. Write these five things on the sticky note and save it with your homeschool records. At the end of each year, group the sticky notes together and combine them to create high school courses.

I recognize it can be hard to determine where each experience will fall on a transcript, so keep each sticky note simple. On each note, indicate each of the following items.

## 1. Name the Experience

In the middle, write the experience. What did your child do? "Perform in the Nutcracker." Do you have any course title ideas, such as "Theatrical performance" or "economics?" Guess—and feel free to guess many times on each sticky note!

## 2. Note the year

When did your child do this? Sometimes it will be a school year, such as 2019-2020, and other times it will be for a short duration, such as a play in November, 2020.

## 3. Grade the experience

Did your student complete the project to your expectations? Were they successful, did they receive positive feedback, or learn something? Remember that you don't have to test to give a grade. You can evaluate them in other ways.

## 4. Note credits earned or hours spent

Count or estimate the number of hours you spent on the project. A total of 75 to 90 hours could be recorded as "1/2 credit" when you are done with the experience. If you have more than 180 hours, you could consider it a full credit, or you might choose to divide up your experiences into smaller bite-sized pieces and then regroup them into other courses with 180 hours apiece. If you have less than 75 hours, you will be grouping the sticky notes together, and I'll describe that in a moment. Keep sticky notes even when the activity required few hours. You can use those experiences no matter how many hours they spend.

## 5. Suggest possible subject areas

You may not know which subjects you will use for each experience but it's helpful to record the possibilities. With all our reports and papers, I would often put several ideas on each note. One paper might be regarded as English, history, economics, or French. By making a note of it, I could decide later which course needed the experience to make up a full credit. If history was already packed, then I would use another subject area.

Spread them out and group them together.

Don't review sticky notes until you are working on the transcript. Checking them too often can cause frustration and insecurity, so only review them when updating the transcript. This will help you keep the big picture in mind. When you are ready to work on the transcript, spread all the sticky notes on the table or floor. Then arrange them into *affinity groups*—groups of similar things. Work to combine them into groups that ultimately add up to one credit or half credit courses.

Include each course on the transcript.

Make a note of the experiences you included on the transcript if you want to. This will help if you decide to add course descriptions to your child's homeschool records later. Once you've decided on a credit, try not to stress about it. It's easy enough to change when you need to, but even arranging experiences into groups is a success. You have successfully grouped your child's delight directed learning into high school level courses!

This whole process of spreading notes out on the floor and manually grouping and regrouping experiences is a great technique for any parent who is a kinesthetic learner. Even if you don't use a hands-on curriculum, this transcript process can help you understand the nuances of your child's transcript and can ultimately help you remember what was included in each course—and even help you write course descriptions! Keep the information with your child's homeschool records.

## The Testing Strategy

Another way to quantify delight directed learning is to give subject tests. This doesn't work for every subject or every child, but it's an option to consider. Instead of testing your child as they are learning, allow them to learn a subject naturally. When they are done, you can give them a sample test from a major test provider. If they pass the sample test at home or at the testing center, you will know how much they have learned, and will have a grade to put on their transcript. There are three tests available that will help you with this strategy: SAT Subject Tests, AP exams, and CLEP tests.

Parents don't always know what their children are learning.

There is so much life that goes on—and so many books! It's amazing what children learn when we aren't looking! Using CLEP exams, I found out how true this could be! I told my students to look over the exams "just to see what they were like." One son was able to pass an exam in Business Law, even though I had never seen a law book in my home. He passed the Principles of Marketing test, even though I had never seen a marketing book in my home. He passed both Microeconomics *and* Macroeconomics, even though I still don't know exactly what those two words mean. By testing my kids, I was able to put some courses on the transcript that were a surprise even to me!

When using tests to document delight directed learning, be sure to avoid failure.

Purchase a book with sample tests in it and give the exam at home first. Only take your student to an official test if you are reasonably sure they can pass it. Your goal is to find out what they have learned, not demonstrate what they have *not* learned. For more information on SAT Subject Tests, AP exams, or the CLEP test, go to CollegeBoard.com.

Chapter 8

# Bonus: Financial Rescue Package

When your commitment to homeschooling is high, but the economy is low, what is a parent to do? It's time to think creatively and brainstorm ideas to help your homeschool thrive even in a difficult economy.

The economic meltdown may be too close for comfort in your home, but there are still some drastic cost-cutting strategies that will help you survive.

## Don't Pay to Play

First, you can save the most money simply by not paying for the privilege to homeschool. Homeschool at home—

don't pay for the joy of homeschooling. You don't have to pay for a co-op class, an accrediting agency, or a homeschool program. They aren't necessary for your success.

Whatever you do, don't Google "free homeschool." All you will get is a bunch of advertisements for government programs that say they are free, when they aren't. The cost of these programs is described in my newsletter article, "Love with Some Strings Attached." Compare your homeschool costs to the cost of public or private education. What a great value homeschooling is, when you don't pay extra for classes outside the home! Don't pay for the privilege of homeschooling. It is an unnecessary expense.

## Buy Smart

Have you noticed that curriculum choices are ever changing, and the grass always seems greener with the *other* choice? Buy smart! Create a new mantra for your shopping. Repeat after me, "I'm looking for tried and true, not latest and greatest." Choosing curriculum that isn't brand new can save a *lot* of money.

Invest first in your weaknesses. If you need help with math, buy a math curriculum first. Invest in your vocation as the teacher and buy high school resources that will teach you what you need to know.

When you shop for your children, buy curriculum made for homeschoolers. Homeschool curriculum assumes you know nothing about the subject matter. If you need help, Cathy Duffy is my favorite curriculum review author. Check out her book, *102 Top Picks For Homeschool Curriculum: Choosing The Right Curriculum And Approach For Your Child's Learning Style.*

## Choosy Mothers Choose Math

Math is a priority, but it is extremely

frustrating when you sacrifice money on a math curriculum that doesn't work for your child. Encourage your child to choose their math. Instead of *guessing* which math curriculum is right for your child, encourage them to help you make the choice. This is especially effective as they approach their teen years and the *style* of the math book or tutorial can start to be important to them.

Compare math programs and invest in a good video tutorial if you aren't 100 percent comfortable. Watch each program's tutorial for Algebra 1, so you are comparing apples to apples. If you want, narrow it down to two or three good choices, each appropriate for your student. Let your child watch each video clip and decide which one they like. Kids are finicky, and you never know for sure which video presentation will drive them crazy. Let them take a test drive to see the video for themselves. It may help you avoid an expensive curriculum failure.

## Go to the Library

Go to the library for the bulk of your curriculum. You can search for fiction, nonfiction, educational videos, and supplemental materials. Many of The Great Courses lectures are available at the library and they are worth their weight in gold. Before there were curriculum providers and tutorials for everything, homeschool families went to the library to learn. While at the library, consider these books to help you with other frugal homeschool ideas.

- *Homeschool Your Child for Free: More Than 1,200 Smart, Effective, and Practical Resources for Home Education on the Internet and Beyond* by Laura Maery Gold and Joan Zielinski

- *Homeschooling on a Shoestring: A Jam-packed Guide* by Melissa Morgan and Judith Waite Allee

If your personal economy is in the tank,

you don't have to buy a curriculum for most subjects if you can do it for almost nothing. One of my favorite writing resources is a small, inexpensive $10 book called *501 Writing Prompts*. I recommend it all the time because it's simple, inexpensive, and part of why my child got a perfect score on the SAT essay.

Since the book is under $10, this may be a *great* year to study essay writing. You can dig deeper into essay writing as well. One year, I searched for scholarship essays for my children. They spent the year writing scholarship essays for their writing plan.

Learning can take place outside of a curriculum. A lifestyle of learning can be taught this way—it's a good thing, not a weakness.

**Get a Job**

Some families are faced with the necessity of the homeschool parent returning to work. If you are in this position, remember that your goal is for your children to become self-taught. If they learn on their own because you aren't there to teach them, it's a *good* thing! Use a self-teaching homeschool curriculum that doesn't require your help. Getting a job may force your child into independent learning but being self-taught is a valuable skill.

Families with two working parents can find solutions that work. You can share the work with your spouse and alternate your days or hours working out of the home. This is a great idea if you have an unreliable teenager, a young child at home, or a large family. You could share your homeschool work with a homeschool friend. Single parent homeschoolers often use this strategy, as they partner with another single parent.

Another option is to study entrepreneurship with your high school student and work from home. You can have your teenager complete a unit study on entrepreneurship at www.microbusinessforteens.com.

Occupational education can be included on the homeschool transcript. Meanwhile, adding these business skills to the core subjects can improve your ability to work at home, add income to the family, and teach valuable skills in occupational education.

## Compensate with Thorough Record Keeping

You can compensate for a lot when you prepare careful documentation of your homeschool. Colleges need a transcript and you can make it yourself. Colleges like to see a reading list as well. It helps them evaluate each student during the admission process. Course descriptions are important as well.

Although a transcript and reading list are a good start, many colleges rely on course descriptions to understand your homeschool. In a simple paragraph, you can describe delight directed learning and self-taught courses. Course descriptions can include all the library books your child read, every video and audio supplement, and each free museum pass, and demonstrate a quality education without the use of a prepared curriculum or outside courses. Careful course descriptions with carefully chosen high school tests can provide educational jargon for life experience and library learning. It takes effort to research high school tests and write course descriptions, but both can save you a lot of money in the long run. My Total Transcript Solution and Comprehensive Record Solution can help you with these tasks.

## Think, Don't Panic

Even in a difficult economy, the benefits of homeschooling are clear. Don't pay for the privilege of homeschooling.

Spend your money wisely. Invest in the difficult subjects and use the library for the rest. Think creatively if you need to work outside the home. Most importantly, *do not panic*. Take a deep breath, study your options, and act with confidence.

Appendix 1

# Complete the FAFSA for Fun and Profit

## Enjoy a Fun New Fall Tradition

FAFSA stands for "Free Application for Federal Student Aid." It's a form you fill out, much like 1040 tax forms. Like the tax forms, these are also super-fun and well-written government prose. The U.S. Department of Education requires the FAFSA to receive any government money for college. They mean "free" because it doesn't cost money to apply for the money. It does *not* mean hassle-free, however. This form is how the government conducts a need analysis with information from your income tax forms. This need analysis determines your Expected Family Contribution

(EFC) or *how much you can afford.* (Yes, insert laugh track here.)

Would you prefer to get *one* year of money for college, or *four* years of money for college? That's good news! Because you must fill out the form for every year of college to get the money! Thank goodness we love these forms so much! For added fun, your EFC, or *how much you can afford* is based on the income of the entire family, and both parents. This can make it awkward or complicated if you are separated or divorced.

Now correct me if I'm wrong here, but the government is *not* a bottomless pit of money. The government has a limited supply of funds. This money they provide for college is first-come, first served. I humbly suggest that you place yourself first in line. Be first in line each year you want money, too.

The first time you need to fill out these

fun forms is during your eldest child's senior year. You must fill out these forms every year until your youngest graduates from college, for as long as you have a child attending college the following year.

You have plenty of time to be completely comfortable with this required paperwork. You're completely confident when you fill out your taxes each year, right? And, sadly, this is no different. They need a new form every year. Every. Single. Year.

## Filling Out the FAFSA

To fill out the FAFSA, you need a super-secure, top secret, special FSA ID. As you know, the government is a stickler - they are that concerned about secure information. You can request your life-long FSA ID at studentaid.ed.gov/sa/fafsa/filling-out/fsaid. You'll need an ID for your child and for the parents. To receive an FSA ID, you will need these basic tools found around your home: your Social Security Number, your Alien Registration Number (if not a citizen), your most recent Federal Income Tax Returns, W-2s, other records of money earned, recent bank statements, records of investments, and records of untaxed income. I'm sure you can tell already how much fun this yearly task will be.

Just as you use your Social Security Number for tax returns, you also must provide it for federal loans. In this instance, the Social Security Number is important. The information must be the same for both the FAFSA and your income tax returns. The right hand does know what the left hand is doing, so you must make sure your numbers are the same for your tax forms as for your financial aid forms.

The FAFSA is supposed to tell you how much you can afford to pay for college. Wouldn't it be nice to know how much Uncle Sam thinks you can pay? The government has a fun game you can play, much like the Magic 8 Ball, called the FAFSA Forecaster. If you go to the FAFSA4caster at fafsa.ed.gov/FAFSA/app/f4cForm, you can estimate your eligibility for federal student aid. Please remember this is federal and it is aid. This is money you could receive directly from the federal government. It does not include scholarship awards that you might get from colleges. This is not how much colleges will give you, or how much you can receive in full tuition scholarships. Those big awards come from colleges who are, frankly, much better at handling their money, so they have more money to give away.

The FAFSA is also about financial aid, not a financial windfall. Much of the money will come to you as a loan you have to repay, or as a work study that assumes the student is working for minimum wage. Your estimate will be shown in the "College Cost Worksheet" where you can also provide estimated amounts of other student aid and savings you have that can go towards your college education. Guessing is hard, since you haven't applied yet, and may not even know which colleges you want to attend.

## FAFSA Tips

Efficiency is key, as it is obviously an important component in all areas of the federal government. Unfortunately, you can't plan and gradually ease into the FAFSA. Although January 1st used to be the first day you could see the forms, now you can begin filling them out on October 1st. You will simply use your tax information from the previous year (no waiting to collect tax info to complete the FAFSA as was the case in the past).

I'm not going to sugar-coat this; I'm not very good at filling out government forms. You might say I was even petrified of the FAFSA. Even though I'm the designated tax preparer of my family, I was still completely baffled. I'm sure it will be much, much easier for you, though. Since I filled out the form years ago, I understand that they have vastly improved the entire process. With this new and improved process, the U.S. Secretary of Education says the FAFSA is "still a real pain in the assets." As you can tell, this is a huge improvement over previous versions which were also declared "a huge pain in the assets."

Many short videos have been made to help you through the process. If you search for How to Fill Out Your FAFSA, you'll find some assistance. The federal government has a series of videos to help on YouTube, called "FAFSA: Apply for Aid."

It's possible that I have a bad attitude about tax-related forms. It's possible that I might have inadvertently shared my dismay, and influenced you in a negative way, causing you to dread the coming task. I encourage you to muscle past the gag reflex and learn to love it. It's part of your destiny!

There is no time like the present. Embrace change. Good things come to those who work hard and pull themselves up by the bootstraps. I hope this information has helped you today, or if nothing else, has given you a smirk or a smile as you consider your future.

Your mission, should you choose to accept it:

*Complete the FAFSA in October of senior year.*

## Vocabulary Words

- FAFSA: Free Application for Federal Student Aid

- EFC: Expected Family Contribution

- Grants: Money they give you

- Loans: Money you must repay

- Work Study: Money you must work for and earn, usually at minimum wage

## Executive Summary

## Begin a NEW Fall Tradition

- Complete the FAFSA on October 1st of senior year

- Complete the FAFSA on October 1st every year until your youngest graduates college

**The Carrot:** federal grants, loans, and work-study for college or trade schools often worth thousands of dollars.

**The Stick:** filing deadlines depends on the school but could be the first weeks in January. Missing deadlines can ruin chances for financial aid.

**The Exception:** some colleges don't use the FAFSA or accept any federal funding. When you receive great financial aid, it may eclipse federal aid and make filling out those forms unnecessary.

Appendix 2

# 9 Secrets to Effortlessly Finish the FAFSA

What's more fun than completing your taxes? Filling out the FAFSA, of course! The FAFSA is a source of college scholarships, and it must be completed by college-bound seniors and their parents. So, if your child is headed to college, complete the FAFSA during October of senior year.

With the new changes made to the FAFSA this year, some may find it easier to complete than in years past, but certainly not more fun. There are two key changes to the FAFSA, and nine simple steps for getting it done.

There are three things you need to know about the process before you get started.

1. Start the FAFSA October 1st

October should now be known as the month you have to fill out the FAFSA. Don't delay! To get the best financial aid available to you, fill out this form as soon as possible after October 1st. Plan to fill it out every year from senior year in high school until your student is finished with college.

2. Use Last Year's Tax Return

Instead of estimating taxes, you will use last year's tax returns. The tax return you use to fill out the FAFSA is the most recent federal tax return you filed. For example, in October of 2016, use your tax returns from 2015.

3. Collect Your Documents

To fill out the FAFSA, you will need:

- Your Social Security Number

- Your most recent federal income tax returns, W-2s, and any other records of money earned

- Bank statements and records of investments (if applicable)

- Records of untaxed income (if applicable)

- An FSA ID to sign the form electronically. If you don't have an ID, you will be given the option to register for one at the end of the process, before you are able to sign electronically. (Note: Your student needs one too). You can register for an FSA ID prior to beginning at https://fsaid.ed.gov/npas/index.htm.

Ready? Let's dig in and finish that FAFSA!

**Step 1 - The Process**

Go to www.fafsa.ed.gov to get started. You will have the option to start a new FAFSA or to login as a returning user. If you have already filled out or started your FAFSA form this year, but haven't submitted it yet, you can login to pick up where you left off. You can start and save the FAFSA for up to 45 days.

For the purposes of this article, we will assume you are starting a new FAFSA. If you are filling out the FAFSA for your student, choose the "Enter Student's Information" option on the login page. Once you click this button, boxes will show up asking for the student's name, social security number, and the student's date of birth. When all is said and done, this application should take you about an hour to fill out.

You will be asked to verify that you entered your student's information correctly. If you have, simply click the "Next" arrow.

## Step 2 - Getting Started

Once you have confirmed the information is correct, you will be taken to a page that asks which year you are applying for aid. Click the year you are applying for. You will be asked to "Create a Save Key." This is a numeric password used in case you need to come back to finish, or to log back in if you leave your screen for 10 minutes or more. Click the "Next" arrow.

The next page is an introduction page with FAQs. There is helpful information here, so spend a second or two reading it over. Each blue link is clickable. After you finish reading, click the "Next" arrow to move on.

## Step 3 - Student Demographic Section

Now, here's where we get into the nitty-gritty of the FAFSA. First is the student section. (Don't worry parents ... your turn is coming!) The first page of this section is straightforward, asking for mailing address, phone number, email, etc. After you have filled this out, click the "Next" arrow. Student Eligibility comes next. Still nothing too difficult here. Fairly straightforward.

There are two sections in Student Eligibility. The second section asks for the name of your student's high school. No need to be formal or fancy here, simply type "homeschool," fill in the city and state, and confirm. After hitting the "confirm" button, a list of high school choices will pop up at the bottom. Homeschool will not be listed, simply click the "Next" arrow.

## Step 4 - School Selection

On this screen, you will see a couple of boxes at the top alerting you that your student may be eligible for student aid and that the application was successfully saved (hopefully!). That's good! If you don't see these boxes, you will have to go back and fix whatever didn't go quite right the first time. Here, you'll add the schools where you want to direct your financial aid. You can list up to 10, either by searching their state, city, or school name. Alternatively, if you know the school's federal school code, you can enter it.

Once you search for a school, a list of colleges (only one if you entered a code or a specific name) will come up. Click on the box to the left of the school you want to receive your information and click "Add." The school information will be automatically entered in the box on the right of the screen. When you see it there, click the "Next" arrow.

The next page allows you the opportunity to view the selected school information but is mostly a confirmation that you are happy with the school(s) you have chosen. Don't forget to select the housing option in the drop-down box. You still have the option to add more schools to your list if you haven't already used all 10 spaces allotted for school choices. Click the "Next" arrow.

## Step 5 - Dependency Status

You've reached a new section! Again, you should see a box come up at the top stating your application was successfully saved. If you don't see this statement, you'll need to go fix what went wrong. More straightforward questions ... however, this is one of two pages where more questions will continue to come up as you answer questions, depending upon your answers. Hang in there and keep answering.

If your student is determined to be a dependent student, you will have to provide parental information through filling out the first part of this form. There are two options on this screen: to provide parental information or not provide parental information. If you choose to provide information, you'll be taken to the Parent Demographics section. If you choose not to provide parental information, you will see a page that explores the "why," with three options to choose from.

## Step 6 - Parent Demographics Information

"Application was successfully saved" should be displayed at the top of the page! If it is, proceed to filling out the requested information. This is a tricky page because the page changes depending on the option you choose for your marital status. For some options, it only asks for single parent information, for other options, it asks for information on both parents.

And, just when you were getting comfortable and thinking this was a breeze, it gets tricky. The next section is the dreaded tax forms.

## Step 7 - Parent Tax Information

Although some will resist it, there is an option for most people to connect to the IRS site and pull your tax information directly from it. It is much easier to do it this way, but it is understandable if you choose not to. I say, "for most people," because if you have filed a Form 1040X amended tax return or filed in Puerto Rico in 2015, you cannot link to the IRS.

You do need your FSA ID to link to the IRS site. If you choose to link to the IRS site, you'll be asked to fill in your address to pull information. It pulls up your name, social security number, date of birth, and filing status automatically, (depending on if you use parent one or parent two's FSA ID). You will also need to click the "Transfer" button at the bottom of the tax information. If you get this far and panic, there is a button for not transferring information as well.

This section can get sticky if you don't link because some of the numbers they want are unclear, especially if you are filling in information for two parents. It can be done but is the more difficult option. This is the second page that continues to add questions as you answer the previous one.

If you have chosen to transfer your tax information, you will see another box at the top of the screen (once you are transferred back to the FAFSA website) saying you have successfully done so. For this page and the next, you must trust you can do it! I can't show you screen shots of these due to private financial information.

## Step 8 - Student Tax Information

This section is much like the previous section on parent taxes. If your child has worked and received W-2s, then this will apply. If they haven't, you'll be entering many zeroes. Unfortunately, you still must fill it out.

Much like the parent tax information, you will likely have the option to connect to the IRS site and transfer data from their site. Again, it is the easier option, but if you choose not to for the child, it is easier to fill out the tax information manually in this section.

Fill in the financial information over the next two pages for your student. Hang in there; you're getting close to the end!

## Step 9 - Sign & Submit

This is the last section you will need to fill out, and it is the easiest. Remember that FSA ID you made at the beginning? Now you need to pull it out. To electronically sign the form and submit it, you'll need this ID. You are encouraged not to sign for your child. They will need to help you make their FSA ID to use as their own electronic signature.

There are two other options for submitting the FAFSA. You can print and mail the signature page or submit it without signatures. The printing and mailing option obviously takes a little longer. Submitting without signatures allows you to submit it if your student isn't around at the time, but you will still have to return later to sign it before it is officially submitted.

Answer the few questions there, read the "Read before proceeding" box, "sign" your name and have your student "sign" their name. After the signatures are complete, click the "Submit my FAFSA now" button. That's it! Now, wasn't that easy?

In the end . . .

After you submit your FAFSA, you will have the option to print the document on the ending page. It is helpful to print a copy and save a copy on your computer. You will also get an email confirming you have submitted your FAFSA form successfully. If you're curious, about halfway down the email you will find estimated eligibility criteria and, if you have qualified, the amount the government expects you will receive in financial aid. This isn't a definitive answer on your qualification, only an estimate.

After you click the "Exit" button in the bottom right, you will see the final screen.

Here are a couple of tips before I leave you to your computer and FAFSA form.

1. If there is a problem throughout the process, the program will tell you. If you click the "Next" button and there is an error, it will not allow you to continue until the error is fixed.

2. If you have questions, there is a help box on the right side of each page. You won't always find the answer you're looking for, but there are answers to general questions.

3. There is a "Save" button at the bottom of each page. If you are in the middle of filling out your FAFSA and life happens, don't panic! Save it and come back to it later.

Congratulations! You are now an experienced FAFSA enthusiast! Well, OK, maybe not. But next year when you come back, you'll know exactly what to expect having experienced the process before.

Afterword

# Who is Lee Binz and What Can She Do for Me?

Number one best-selling homeschool author, Lee Binz is The HomeScholar. Her mission is "helping parents homeschool high school." Lee and her husband, Matt, homeschooled their two boys, Kevin and Alex, from elementary through high school.

Upon graduation, both boys received four-year, full tuition scholarships from their first choice university. This enables Lee to pursue her dream job—helping parents homeschool their children through high school.

On The HomeScholar website, you will find great products for creating homeschool transcripts and comprehensive records to help you amaze and impress colleges.

Find out why Andrew Pudewa, Founder of the Institute for Excellence in Writing says, "Lee Binz knows how to navigate this often confusing and frustrating labyrinth better than anyone."

You can find Lee online at:

### HomeHighSchoolHelp.com

If this book has been helpful, could you please take a minute to write us a quick review on Amazon? Thank you!

# Testimonials

## She literally checked every box on my list . . . and then some!

*Thank You*, Lee! After many hours of sitting at my laptop trying to create the "perfect" *high school transcript*, I googled and found Lee's website. What a relief! Within minutes of chatting online with a consultant, I purchased the (very reasonably priced) Total Transcript Solution packet which gave me instant access to numerous transcript templates and an online tutorial video!

Questions? What questions! She literally checked every box on my list . . . and then some! Within an hour, I had completed the transcript and printed a draft copy (thanks to my thorough record keeping.) What a blessing! You won't be disappointed, I promise. If you're doing transcripts, The Total Transcript Solution is the way to go!

~Carol

---------

## I only wish I would have ordered sooner!

Lee's teaching and training is phenomenal as well as easy to follow! She brings comfort and capability to the mom who may feel stressed in light of the daunting responsibility of homeschooling high school. A few years ago, Lee's free webinar with Dr. Jay Wile, "Homeschooling, How and Why it Works" gave my husband and I the courage to start homeschooling high school for our oldest daughter and over the last few years I have listened numerous times to Lee's free webinars on how to prepare transcripts and complete records.

I just ordered the Comprehensive Record Solution and it feels like a breath of fresh air after having crafted my oldest daughter's records on my own. The Comprehensive Record Solution provides the preformatted templates for the *entire* comprehensive record, as well as training and help. It's quite amazing. Keeping records for my next oldest daughter, who starts high school in the fall, will be a breeze. I only wish I would have ordered the Comprehensive Record Solution sooner!

~ Joelle

For more information about my **Total Transcript Solution** and **Comprehensive Record Solution**, go to:

www.TotalTranscriptSolution.com
www.ComprehensiveRecordSolution.com

# Also From
# The HomeScholar...

- The HomeScholar Guide to College Admission and Scholarships: Homeschool Secrets to Getting Ready, Getting In and Getting Paid (Book and Kindle Book)

- Setting the Records Straight—How to Craft Homeschool Transcripts and Course Descriptions for College Admission and Scholarships (Book and Kindle Book)

- TechnoLogic: How to Set Logical Technology Boundaries and Stop the Zombie Apocalypse

- Finding the Faith to Homeschool High School

- Parent Training A la Carte (Online Training)

- Total Transcript Solution (Online Training, Tools and Templates)

- Comprehensive Record Solution (Online Training, Tools and Templates)

- High School Solution (Online Training, Tools, Resources, and Support)

- College Launch Solution (Online Training, Tools, Resources, and Support)

- Gold Care Club (Comprehensive Online Support and Training)

- Silver Training Club (Online Training)

# The HomeScholar Coffee Break Books Released or Coming Soon on Kindle and Paperback:

- Delight Directed Learning: Guiding Your Homeschooler Toward Passionate Learning

- Creating Transcripts for Your Unique Child: Help Your Homeschool Graduate Stand Out from the Crowd

- Beyond Academics: Preparation for College and for Life

- Planning High School Courses: Charting the Course Toward High School Graduation

- Graduate Your Homeschooler in Style: Make Your Homeschool Graduation Memorable

- Keys to High School Success: Get Your Homeschool High School Started Right!

- Getting the Most Out of Your Homeschool This Summer: Learning just for the Fun of it!

- Finding a College: A Homeschooler's Guide to Finding a Perfect Fit

- College Scholarships for High School Credit: Learn and Earn With This Two-for-One Strategy!

- College Admission Policies Demystified: Understanding Homeschool Requirements for Getting In

- A Higher Calling: Homeschooling High School for Harried Husbands (by Matt Binz, Mr. HomeScholar)

- Gifted Education Strategies for Every Child: Homeschool Secrets for Success

- College Application Essays: A Primer for Parents

- Creating Homeschool Balance: Find Harmony Between Type A and Type Zzz...

- Homeschooling the Holidays: Sanity Saving Strategies and Gift Giving Ideas

- Your Goals this Year: A Year by Year Guide to Homeschooling High School

- Making the Grades: A Grouch-Free Guide to Homeschool Grading

- High School Testing: Knowledge That Saves Money

- Getting the BIG Scholarships: Learn Expert Secrets for Winning College Cash!

- Easy English for Simple Homeschooling: How to Teach, Assess and Document High School English

- Scheduling—The Secret to Homeschool Sanity: Plan You Way Back to Mental Health

- Junior Year is the Key to High School Success: How to Unlock the Gate to Graduation and Beyond

- Upper Echelon Education: How to Gain Admission to Elite Universities

- How to Homeschool College: Save Time, Reduce Stress and Eliminate Debt

- Homeschool Curriculum That's Effective and Fun: Avoid the Crummy Curriculum Hall of Shame!

- Comprehensive Homeschool Records: Put Your Best Foot Forward to Win College Admission and Scholarships

- Options After High School: Steps to Success for College or Career

- How to Homeschool 9th and 10th Grade: Simple Steps for Starting Strong!

- Senior Year Step-by-Step: Simple Instructions for Busy Homeschool Parents

- How to Homeschool Independently: Do-it-Yourself Secrets to Rekindle the Love of Learning

- High School Math The Easy Way: Simple Strategies for Homeschool Parents in Over Their Heads

- Homeschooling Middle School with Powerful Purpose: How to Successfully Navigate 6th through 8th Grade

- Simple Science for Homeschooling High School: Because Teaching Science isn't Rocket Science!

Would you like to be notified when we offer the next *Coffee Break Books* for FREE during our Kindle promotion days?

If so, leave your name and email below and we will send you a reminder.

HomeHighSchoolHelp.com/
freekindlebook

## Visit my Amazon Author Page!
amazon.com/author/leebinz

Made in the USA
Columbia, SC
24 January 2022

54109574R00059